The Angels of Fortune

Magick for Enrichment, Passion, and Triumph

Rose Manning

Contents

The Angels of Fortune

When I'm looking for an answer, I seek guidance from angels, and that is how I came to call this book *The Angels of Fortune*. It's a word that has many meanings, but here I feel that it means these angels can bring you good fortune in all forms. This magick can help you triumph over adversity, overcome your own shortcomings, or attract the wealth, love, passion, control, and guidance that you long for. It is magick that can make you prosper.

It's quite normal to write the opening of a book at the very end of the quest, and as I write these final words in July of 2019, I have not seen these angels described in any of the popular magick books that have graced contemporary bookshelves. The angels are known by several names, but most often they are called The Thirty-Six Angels of The Decans or The Angels of Decans. What that means will become easy to understand, and you will see why I have come to know them as The Angels of Fortune.

The magick I provide you with is safe, easy to use, and can bring the change and results you need. It doesn't take long to get used to this magick, and it works by combining magickal letters, angelic sigils, divine names, a unique list of Sensory Triggers, and an order of archangels that rule these particular angels. There is no complicated equipment to buy, and there are no difficult techniques, but you will perform a ritual that brings this all together. If you know a lot about magick, this should be new material, and if it is your first magick book, your life is about to change.

Finding out anything about these angels requires detective work, intuition, and magickal exploration. As magick books have grown in popularity, with new books being published every month, I felt certain somebody would explore this subject before I could finish my book. I did not want to work too fast because this is a rich art, and I have spent many years trying to perfect this book for you.

When I first discovered these angels, it felt as though I was being granted the right, privilege, and even the obligation, to share this magick with you. I am so pleased to have reached this day.

In 2014 I wrote a short book about archangels and shared what I was learning about magick. At that time, I thought of it as an expression of The Law of Attraction because I was experienced with angels but new to the concept of magick itself, and only just starting to discover what magick can bring into your life. Angels were familiar to me, but magick was new.

I have come so far since that day, and now believe that magick gives you the power to make the changes you want and need. I want to share that expansion of knowledge with you and help you discover what it is like to work magick with The Angels of Fortune.

By the time my first book was published in 2015, I had already discovered the first steps on this new pathway into magick. I felt blessed to discover and understand something new about these hidden angels, but it has taken many years to gain enough experience to share what I know. It would have been irresponsible to share the knowledge until it was complete.

My journey would have been impossible without a series of beautiful coincidences, chance meetings, and deep experiences. It's been five years since I began to explore the thirty-six angels you will read about here, and every day I have learned something useful. I hope you can feel that experience coming through in my words, and that you benefit from the mistakes I made and the lessons I learned.

I could not have made this journey alone. I have been guided by the angels themselves, by the work of great authors, and by those who were willing to mentor me and guide me to the documents and techniques I needed to sustain my research. Without the trust of those who knew far more than me, I could not have written this book.

I have also looked through the research that's available online, and although astrology is covered satisfactorily, these angels are not. What information you find online is often an unreliable compilation or a series of guesses, and unless it's an extremely reputable site (of which there are very few), you should always back up research with good books, and the knowledge of the experienced. I hope this book will be the only book you need to know about the powers of these angels and the secret method used for calling them.

I have always chosen to use magick that works, and in finding what works, I have been able to direct my attention to the best sources of reliable and effective material.

I am indebted to those who helped me directly, but also to contemporary authors such as Damon Brand, who led the way in creating a new style of practical magick. His work has been copied (and sometimes virtually plagiarized) by many authors, because it is an effective way to communicate the essential techniques of magick without the cluttered musings of opinionated occultists. His books show you how to do magick. I hope to emulate his clarity without stealing any of the content or riding on the coattails of his success. I intend to do that by revealing the power of The Angels of Fortune.

These angels are closely linked to astrology, but you don't need to be an expert in astrology to work with them. You only need to get a feeling for the symbolism of astrology, and I will explain everything you need.

If you know nothing about angels, magick, or astrology, the methods will be revealed in a few short chapters, and that will be all you need to enter the magickal experience.

I trust that you will obtain a response from the angels. The magick will then be yours, and it is my sincere belief that you will feel the loving power of these angels, and you will sense how they can bring improvements to all areas of your life. I believe you will discover that these are angels of great wonder and great fortune.

The Conundrum of The Stars

These angels are closely associated with astrology, but my approach has been to see the astrological correspondences as a way of understanding the angels' powers. The astrological connection does not govern when you can perform the magick.

To show what this means, I can tell you that the angel Losanahar is found in the First Decan of Leo, and has the astrological correspondence Saturn in Leo. But you can work with the angel at any time of the year. You do not need to wait for any pattern in the sky, regarding Saturn and Leo. The correspondence is a description of the angel's power, not a factor that limits when you can use a ritual.

If you are particularly interested in astrology, you may find it useful to employ your knowledge in understanding the underlying correspondences. When you read that the angel Shehadani has the correspondence of Mars in Gemini, you may have an immediate understanding of what that means, and you could work on certain timings if you believe that will help the work. But I always planned to make this book work for readers who have no understanding of astrology, and therefore to see that the Decans are not prisons for the angels, but a beautiful way of determining and recognizing their powers.

If all this talk of Decans is confusing, here's a taste of the background information. A Decan is a measurement found in astrology. If you take the circle of the zodiac, it is divided into twelve sections of thirty degrees each. These sections each represent a sign, such as Cancer, Leo, Virgo, or Gemini. These are the signs that *everybody* is familiar with, but you can split each sign into three Decans, of ten degrees each. The first Decan of a sign is known as the Ascendant, the second as the Succedent, and the third Decan for each sign is known as the Cadent Decan. For simplicity, I call these the First, Second, and Third Decans.

Each of the thirty-six-angels is linked to one of the thirty-six Decans. Mishpar, for example, describes the angel of the Third Decan of Virgo, meaning it has the correspondence of Mercury in Virgo. If you know astrology, you know this will mean there will be attributes such as good planning and decision-making. This is backed up by good observation and reasoning, that may lead to more purpose and energy.

The powers listed for Mishpar in this book come from those correspondences. Sometimes, for some angels, there are additional powers that are less obvious, but they rarely stray far from those that are suggested by astrology. I have seen some fanciful writing that suggests other powers attributed to the angels, but these appear to be based on wishful thinking and have not proven to be successful with long-term practice. If you use the powers I reveal, they should make sense, and they should work. All powers can be adapted, of course. The powers of Mishpar could be effective in business, in relationships, and in so many areas of life. But I have chosen to describe the powers honestly and conservatively, rather than making claims that might sell more books, but that won't be helpful to you.

If you are completely unfamiliar with astrology, then you should know that as well as the twelve signs of the zodiac, there are 'planets' of The Sun (Sol), The Moon (Luna), Mercury, Venus, Mars, Jupiter, and Saturn. Modern astrology added Uranus, Neptune, and Pluto when they were discovered, but the traditional approach is effective for these angels.

Each sign and each planet are connected to various powers, sometimes described as aptitudes, abilities, and areas of influence. When these are combined, you get a quite specific range of powers that can be used in your magick. By looking at the correspondences for an angel of the Decans, you can make a good guess as to its powers. I have done this for you, so that you don't have to learn any astrological details.

The Decans are a useful way of ordering the angels and understanding how the blend of their powers work. For me, as a researcher and experiencer, the Decans were essential, but for you, understanding the nature of each angel and what it can bring to your life will be more important than any of that astrological detail.

It took me a long time, but I discovered that these angels are not constrained by dates and times, as I first thought, but their powers are described by the beautiful symbolism of astrology. This brings great freedom to the magick, because you don't need to be limited by your date of birth, the time of year, or the hour of the day. The astrological aspects of this work are descriptions that bring clarity and beauty to the angelic work, without adding restraints or complications.

Partly this is because there isn't a single astrology, and some orders have their own way of measuring and describing the zodiac. When I said earlier that Tarasni is connected to The Sun in Libra, not everybody would agree. And this is the conundrum faced when decoding these angelic powers.

When it comes to The Angels of Fortune, is astrology everything, or nothing? One occultist I know said the answer to that was 'both,' which felt unhelpful at first, but gave me some mystical insight. It led me to find the correspondences that produced an effective connection to the angels, with magickal results that make sense.

Although astrology may seem like a set of mathematical certainties, it is a very fluid system, with myriad interpretations. There are long-running arguments about whether the first degrees of the zodiac are marked from Aries or from Leo, and even putting that aside, there are several versions of astrology from more ancient times and various cultures, along with modern revisions. Some of these revisions are based on new research, and some are made for convenience. The result is that astrology can be quite confusing.

It is particularly confusing when you look at The Angels of The Decans. Of the few widely available books that list the Decans, there are many contradictions. *The Complete Magician's Tables* by Stephen Skinner, shows one of these contradictions, by displaying the 'traditional' correspondences, above those used by The Golden Dawn (a famous and influential Magickal Order that helped bring magick to the West). The correspondences in each table are quite different, so which are we to use? If I get it wrong, none of this will make sense for you.

My way of working was to experiment with the angels until I recognized a pattern (being guided by my mentors), and discovered which sources were the most reliable. It was interesting to find that certain sources were accurate in some areas, but not in others. For you, as a reader wanting to use magick, I can relieve you of the pressure of trying to work out what is right, because I have done the research and found the correspondences that not only make apparent sense, but that work. The short answer is that the traditional table has proven to be the most accurate, overall, with one or two errors. The Golden Dawn offered many workable insights, and indeed there were variations within their papers and notes, but the traditional approach (which may have been in use when people first worked with these angels) is generally the most effective for this magick.

If you compare the astrology in this book to something from a popular astrology text, it might look like I've messed everything up, but that's because those books often include the modern planets and use The Golden Dawn correspondences. It's important to know there are alternatives, and for these ancient angels, those alternatives are the ones we use.

I believe that putting too much attention on the astrological aspect of the angels could be confusing to many readers, and could limit the usefulness of the magick. I will even say that there are some respected occultists who say these angels have no significant connection to astrology other than one imposed on them to make understanding their powers easier. I do not agree with this, but I do not include astrological symbols in the angelic seals and I offer no methods for timing your rituals according to the stars. This is a benefit, not a burden, and although The Angels of the Decans are, to me undoubtedly inspired by and connected to powers and energies familiar to people with an understanding of astrology, the angels will respond to your magickal call whenever you choose to perform a ritual. The powers listed in this book will work as they are described.

There is one small and notable exception to all this. Earlier I said that the Decans are not a factor that limits when the angel can be contacted through ritual. This is true, but there are specific days that are more effective for each of the angels. Mishpar, for example, will be most effective if you perform the ritual on a Wednesday. But it is not essential.

I give these key days for each angel, but it is really important you don't let this limit your work. By working on a specific day, you are perfecting the ritual and maximizing all known aspects that could improve the working. But this does not mean you should only work the magick on the 'correct' day. There is no 'correct' day but an *ideal* day. If you can only do magick on a Saturday, then do the magick on Saturday, whatever the angel.

Performing magick is more important than waiting for the right day. This is a small aspect of this system, and I was tempted to leave it out of the book because I know some people may believe that they have to get every detail right. I have included this as an option, so you can perfect the magick if it suits your circumstances. If not, work on any day.

It is also worth mentioning the confusion that can arise by mixing in the Tarot cards, because you may find these angels being connected to the Tarot.

According to some authors, such as Aleister Crowley, each angel is associated with a Tarot card. The Tarot is a rich and fascinating subject, but I believe the connections are weak, and sometimes unhelpful. If you look at Crowley's attributions, using the example of the angel Mishpar, he says that the Ten of Pentacles is the correct Tarot card. This doesn't make sense when you look at everything else we know about the angel. The Ten of Pentacles most often represents wealth, and we know from studying the astrological aspects of Mercury in Virgo that wealth is not the main power of Mishpar. The angel could be asked to assist with some aspects of attaining wealth, but would only be effective when using the powers of planning, observation, and decision-making that are true to the angel. The Tarot attributions can make it too easy to jump to the wrong conclusion about these angels and their powers.

In some cases, Crowley lists a main attribute that is reasonably accurate, but it doesn't usually tie in with the traditional attributes of the assigned Tarot card. This implies that there was an effort to forcefully attach the Tarot to these angels (perhaps because Crowley loved the Tarot) and not because there is an intrinsic connection.

After extensive testing, I have found that the Tarot connections are not accurate enough to be reliable. You may get a result when you use them, but I think that is more down to the force of belief that can empower short-term magick, and not due to the authentic powers of the angels. These are the Angels of The Decans, and although I have downplayed the importance of astrology in working with them, it is important to know that they are not Angels of Tarot.

I have also found that all methods for using the Tarot to contact the angels are ineffective. Drawing out the 'appropriate' card and incorporating it into the ritual has no noticeable effect, and I have come to believe the Tarot associations are loose, and perhaps arbitrary.

If you wish to experiment with the Tarot or research further, the required information can be found at the end of the book, but I do not believe that current attributions contribute to practical magick.

This short introduction to the background history shows there is a beautiful tapestry of meaning associated with the mystery of these angels, but understanding the origins is not vital to you, as a reader, beyond what you have read here. If you want to explore the astrology, you might find out something interesting, but you can begin working with the angels right away. If you have no further interest in astrology, you can leave it behind at this point and perform the ritual as I will explain it to you.

The Magickal Method

When you perform a ritual, you don't need to do anything too unusual, but you will get into a state of mind suitable for magick, you will say words of divine power, and you will use an angelic seal. If you know this already, please read my personal overview of this process as it may be different from other magick you know. If magick is a new experience, I hope this will make it seem less intimidating.

I have provided seals for you, with one for each angel. They look like this:

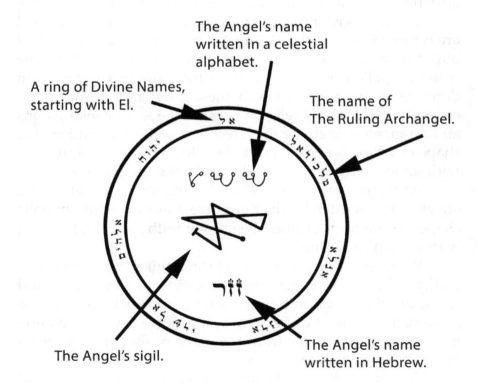

The Angel's name written in a celestial alphabet.

A ring of Divine Names, starting with El.

The name of The Ruling Archangel.

The Angel's sigil.

The Angel's name written in Hebrew.

Magickal seals mix symbolic images (sometimes encoded using a cipher), with divine names and angel names, often written in Hebrew and sometimes written in an angelic script. The long tradition of creating seals in this manner is proven to be one of the factors that can help you make contact with an angel. A seal you construct yourself can work extremely well if you understand the methodology required, but what I give you in this book has been thoroughly researched and tested, so you can trust that it will work.

Each seal is made from a circle containing Hebrew letters. That circle contains divine names and the name of the archangel that rules over the angel you are calling. This sequence of divine names, followed by the archangel name, is an activation sequence for connecting with the angel.

The letters running horizontally across the top of the seal are written in a celestial alphabet. The angel's name is spelled out in an angelic language. At the base of the seal, the same name is spelled out for a second time, now in Hebrew. You don't need to be able to read these languages or have any connection to Hebraic religion because the letter constructions and arrangements create the effect you seek. In occultism, the shape of letters is considered to be a form of practical magick, with some seeing the letters as a spiritual or magickal key.

At the center of the seal is the angel's sigil. This is the angel's name written for the third time, this time with symbolic shapes in the form of lines, beginning with a dot and ending with a small cross-line.

When something is repeated three times, it is urged into reality. Writing the name three times in one language could work, but the variation brings a stronger magick. You see the same name in three different ways, at three levels of reality; from the celestial plane, from the plane of thought, and from the level of ordinary existence.

The sigils are created using complex number squares, and explaining how they work would take several chapters without offering you any benefit, but you may wish to know a little more so that you can understand why a few criss-cross lines have anything to do with angels. In some forms of magick, you set the alphabet out on a square or circular grid, and then draw lines between the letters to spell the angel's name. This is a tried and tested method.

A more advanced version creates large 'number squares' based on the gematria of the angel's name and each letter within the name. Using this square, you draw lines that represent not only the letters but the way each letter relates to the next, and to the name as a whole. With the basic system, a three-letter name might only contain two lines, but when using the advanced system, there are many more lines and strokes spelling out the full symbolism of the angel's name. These sigils are more expressive than most because rather than using one number square for all the angels, each angel has a number square generated from its own name and astrological attributes. This is fascinating and satisfying research to perform, but far beyond the scope of this book to explore in detail.

Each angelic sigil, within the seal, should be seen as a visual key to making contact, but it is the combination of the three versions of the name, surrounded by the circle, that makes this work. An angelic seal makes the connection to an angel much easier to achieve.

The white letters in the black circle are the same words you say during the ritual. You don't need to be able to read or speak Hebrew, and I'll show you an easy way to get the pronunciation flowing beautifully.

The divine names are extremely powerful, and being familiar or unfamiliar with them should not make you underestimate their importance and power. The sound of these words takes you into magick. If you are not religious, or if you belong to a religious tradition where these words don't apply, you can think of them as magickal connections to universal power, God Consciousness, or whatever works for you. If you believe in God, you may think of them as a connection to the magickal aspects of God, a conduit between the heavens and earth. Or you might seem them as the embodiment of your hopes and dreams.

Some of the words are simple, and you might wonder how they could be magickal. The name El, for example, is one short sound, so how can it produce magick? The secret to this is that you say the words with magickal intent. That activates the magick contained within the sounds.

The first words you say are El and the Tetragrammaton, which is often written as YHVH. These words are normally said separately, but I've found they work beautifully when blended. I'll explain in more detail.

El is a name of God that might be 4000 or more years old, predating its appearance and acceptance in more modern religions, and its use in The Bible. Here it is used as a primary sound that connects with your conception of God, or if you have no religion, your connection to the source of creation and existence itself.

The Tetragrammaton (which means 'four letters') is the name of God expressed as four Hebrew letters. These are Yod, He, Vav, and He. When written as their English equivalents, that appears as YHVH, which is seemingly unpronounceable, and in some religions, it is said that the name should not be vocalized. In magick, occultists have found two effective ways to say that name. The first is to say the letter names themselves: Yod, He, Vav, He. More effective, however, is the vocalization that sounds as EE-AH-OH-EH. When spoken quickly, this string of sounds is similar to Yahweh, which is how many people interpret the pronunciation of the Tetragrammaton.

When speaking the first words of this ritual, you say El, YHVH. That is, you say ELL, EE-AH-OH-EH. It may take a few minutes of practice, but you should soon be able to make this sound. The comma shows a slight pause. You could think of it as saying El, Yaweh, but I prefer to think of the sounds, and run them together into the flow of ELL, EE-AH-OH-EH. When chanted for a short while, this sound is like the power switch for a magick ritual. Say these sounds with the intention of performing magick, and you will feel the magick begin.

Elohim is a name of God that has many interpretations, originating from thousands of years ago, and the nature of this name appears to be the power of God to guide others, and in magick this is a call to work with angels. By saying ELL-OH-HEEM, you declare your intention to work with an angel in the ritual.

El Shaddai is the next word, and this is another name of God that is many thousands of years old. It is often translated to mean God Almighty, and in magick it shows that you are working with the very source of creation, and choosing to take part in the creation of your life. You don't need to think about this too much, and will only need to make the sound ELL-SHAD-EYE.

Adonai frequently appears in the Bible and is often interpreted as 'Lord.' In ritual, it is a name that activates your connection to the miraculous properties of magick. You pronounce it as ADD-OH-NIGH, where NIGH rhymes with EYE.

Agla, pronounced as AG-AH-LAH, is an acronym for a Hebrew phrase that means 'You, O Lord, are Mighty forever,' but it has a long history of use in magick, being considered the final key to opening the magickal gateway in your conscious and subconscious minds

There are twelve archangels in this book, ruling over the three angels of the astrological signs. The archangel Malchidiel rules over Aries, and is the ruling archangel of Zazer, Behahemi, and Satonder, who are the angels of the First, Second, and Third Decans of Aries. If that sounds confusing, all you need to know is that the right archangel has been chosen for you to work with.

If you research these angels for yourself, you will find that there is some disagreement over which archangel rules over which Decan, which is unsurprising given what I said earlier about disagreements over the nature of astrology. In some lists, you find the archangel Gabriel rules over Pisces, but here I guide you to work with the archangel Amnitziel. I chose to use the list of archangels provided by Dr. Rudd because experimentation showed it to be the most effective. That was not what I expected, but I could not argue with experience, or the experience of others who tested the magick with me, and the changes in their lives that I witnessed.

Another important part of this magick is a list of Sensory Triggers that help you connect with the angels. For each angel, you will find a series of short descriptions that look like a poem. It is my belief that these Sensory Triggers are as important as the angelic seal. They are usually no more than two lines, but you will feel how reading them can trigger the magick and draw the presence of the angel closer.

In some recently published books, Sensory Triggers such as these have been described as 'evocation keys,' and others have called them 'pathworking.' I do not deny the effectiveness (and popularity!) of those books, but I do not think the word 'pathworking' is helpful in this book. You are not trying to imagine a journey to the angel, but reading a short list of descriptions that contain archetypal qualities that make your connection with the angel much more likely to occur.

The Sensory Triggers are based on the astrological correspondences as well as images traditionally associated with the angels. You will find similar descriptions in other books, but none that are quite the same, and I am thankful for the many forms of guidance I received for this aspect of the magick. I believe you will find that when used in the ritual, as described, this can be the moment when you feel a shiver down the spine as you sense the loving and powerful presence of the angel.

The ritual itself is like many others you may have read, without the need for banishing, cleansing, or extensive preparation.

The ritual is performed only once. In magick, there are some rituals that take many days, and I respect those methods. I do believe, however, that with some angels, if your intention is clear and sincere, once is enough.

If you think you've made a mistake, you can repeat the ritual on the same day, but don't repeat it because you have doubts or fears that it wasn't powerful enough. You will have communicated your request to the angel, and if you've followed the instructions for connecting with the angel, some form of result is inevitable. When you ask for extreme change know that it may come, but it will come with some disruption, or it will come so slowly that you will scarcely notice it. The usual procedure is to use magick to progress in relatively small steps, solving immediate problems, easing the pressure in your life, and gradually and strategically building results to obtain all that you desire.

The Range of Powers

In some occult books, there are tables, with lists of powers that you can choose from. If you're interested in making money, you look for Wealth or Money, and under that heading, you find a list of several angels. It's helpful, but it wouldn't work with this book because there are thirty-six angels, each with quite specific and unique powers, briefly described, so any table would be a repetition of the book's main content.

The easiest way to use this is to read through the powers of all thirty-six angels. They are described briefly because that gives you the potential to interpret them. It is very important for me to leave that freedom for you, instead of giving a list of interesting-sounding powers that stretch plausibility.

Reading about all the powers will take you less than an hour, and it could be one of the best magickal investments you make. You will sense, as you read, how these angels could, can, and will liberate you from the present, and grant you the fortune to choose the future you desire.

When you have chosen the angel you want to call, because of its relevant power, you need to formulate your request. You write this request down so that you can use it in the ritual. You could memorize it, but writing it down makes it feel real. You can throw the paper away when the ritual is over, or if you've written it in a magickal journal, just leave it as a record of your intent.

Writing down your request helps you word it in a clear way, and often helps you to understand what it is that you want to say to the angel, and what you really want to ask for. If you ask for something with a long paragraph of details, there is almost no chance that the magick will work. But if you make a request like, 'I want to negotiate more powerfully over the coming months,' that is direct, clear, and specific. You could even say, 'I want to become a powerful negotiator,' because that takes the time limit away. Unless you really need to add a time limit, magick usually works better without one.

I'll give another example, using one of the powers of Kadamidi. The power is described like this: 'Kadamidi is an angel of courage and perseverance. If you are afraid to make the next move, in any area of life, ask the angel to grant you the required courage.' This might work for you because you know you need the courage to quit your job and go freelance.

How much detail should you add to a request like this? Do you need to talk about the courage you'll need to talk to your boss and your family about quitting? Do you need to ask for the courage that you'll personally experience, which will help you to cope with the pressure of going freelance? Thankfully, keeping it simple is the best way. You could write, 'I want the courage to quit my job so that I can go freelance.'

What you need to avoid is writing something like, 'I want the courage to quit my job, end my relationship, and deal with my neighbors, and find the courage to go freelance, talking to new clients, and being confident enough to meet the people I need to network with.' It's just too much.

The angels are blessed with astounding intelligence and can sense the deeper meaning behind your words, so there is no need to add all the extra details or ask for everything at once. Only add enough detail so that your written request is a reminder of what it is you want when you speak during the ritual.

Many occultists like to phrase their request as a plea to the angels, or simply a request, like, 'I ask that you grant me the courage to quit my job.' I have found this to be effective with many angels, but with this group of angels, there is something more powerful about stating what it is that you want. Your 'request' isn't a request in the normal sense of the word. All you do is make a statement about what it is that you want, as you probably noticed in these examples.

There is a slight twist to this, and that is that when you state what you want, you should say why. The reason doesn't have to be anything too special, but it should be honest. If you are asking for more time off work so you can relax, you should say 'I want more free time so that I can relax.' You don't have to say, 'I want more free time, so I can meditate and discover spirituality,' in the hope this will seem more worthy to the angels. They respond to your desire and what you feel and believe you need, so be honest.

Look for the end result you want. So, if you want to get out of debt, you would say, 'I want to get out of debt so that I can feel free,' or 'I want to get out of debt so I can start saving.' Tell your own truth. This is far, far more powerful than saying, 'I want more money so that I can get out of debt.' Focusing on money is the wrong approach because you're looking at one way to get the result you want, rather than the actual result. The actual result is to be debt-free, so focus on that, not on the money. When you take your focus off the process and look at the end result that you want, that's when you get results.

What if you need more money so that you can afford to travel? You could say, 'I want more spare money so that I can go traveling.' That would be ok if you were certain that a lack of money was the main obstacle preventing you from going traveling. If you are willing to be open-minded, you could say, 'I want to go traveling, so I can feel the freedom I've longed for.' That means the angels could be inventive, and instead of getting more money, you might win a prize, or be invited on a trip, or anything else could happen that means you get to travel. The more creative potential you grant to the angels, the more chance you have of getting a result.

You can word the desire however you want, but I hope these tips have given you enough clues to get started. When you look through the powers and think about what you want, it should be easy to find the most suitable angel for your needs and to think of the result you want. Writing it down will get easier with practice. The more honest you are, the shorter and clearer it will usually be.

In some forms of magick, you command angels, and in others, you ask humbly, but I like this approach because you state your honest need. It doesn't feel conceited, or like you're forcing the angels, because you follow the 'request' with gratitude. The angels do not seek praise, but in feeling your gratitude, they sense your trust, your belief, and your genuine desire for the request you have made. That makes them respond to your call.

You may want to work on several concerns at once, whether they are problems to be solved or goals to be attained. I encourage working on no more than three areas at once. If you have the patience (which I recommend), it's better to work on one ritual with full commitment, and then move on to another at a later time. It makes you focus on the current ritual with great intention. When you subsequently move to another ritual, you automatically let go of the previous ritual, and when you move your focus away from it, the result is more likely to come into being.

You may only feel the need to perform one ritual when you begin, and that may be all you need for some time. Or you may begin to integrate magick into your life, with some rituals overlapping. If you use a lot of magick, I strongly suggest you keep a magickal journal (often known as a personal grimoire), so you know what you did when, what your intentions were, and the results that arise.

You can also take note of signs and synchronicities. Many magickal results come in the form of a moment of truth, or a sign of some kind, or just a feeling that's enough to guide you to what you seek. Magick can also make improbable things happen, and you may find yourself doubting that it could have been the magick. It seems too strange, too unlikely that the world could have changed. Or you may find that change is slow.

If you ask an angel for guidance, which is often a good way to proceed with magick, you may sense answers coming to you during the ritual. More often, answers will come to you in dreams, or like a flash of inspiration out of nowhere, days later. Trust these moments and treasure their wisdom and inspiration.

When there is change or resistance to a ritual, try something else, stepping to one side of your result. If you're seeking money to reduce the pressure at home, and money doesn't come as fast as you want, use a ritual to reduce pressure at home instead. (Sometimes, when you do this, the money turns up anyway, as soon as you stop waiting for it.)

If you try to solve a problem by working harder and harder, you only improve your ability to solve that problem by a small percentage. In some cases, you even make things worse by burning out or overworking. Magick can make the difference, but it works most successfully when you are putting in an effort. Although magick can produce astonishing results from nothing, it is standard occult practice to accept that magick works more effectively when you are doing something to cause change through non-magickal efforts. When you put in your own effort and use magick to back up your efforts, your reality is made changeable. The desires and states you seek are more likely to become real. Consider this in all matters, when working magick.

I also recommend working in secret. Tell nobody what you are doing, until you have your result. Speaking about magick dissipates its energy. When a result happens, you can tell people who would understand, but don't try to convince doubters as you're wasting air.

I called this a book of enrichment, passion, and triumph, and it took me a long time to settle on those words. I wanted to excite you, as a reader, but I didn't want to mislead. When you read through all the powers in this book, you should find they fit with what's described in those words.

Enrichment can mean anything from improving yourself, developing skills, and exploring ambition, through to enriching your life financially. Passion can mean romantic love, but it also refers to the countless powers that can help you to enjoy living with your passions, and the people you are passionate about. Triumph can mean that you hold off evil and send away those who would harm you. It also indicates triumph over your bad habits, and it can mean triumph in work, business, and competition. The words enrichment, passion, and triumph rarely appear in the text, but I believe their meaning is found in the essence of all these angelic powers.

Aim high, but also use rituals for results that are much more likely to happen, so that you have a pleasant mix of chance and possibility. Only do this if you have the time and will. Forced magick, where you feel an obligation to do a ritual, never works in my experience. Enjoy the magick, trust that it will work, and it will work.

The Ritual of Fortune

These are the instructions for the ritual itself, and it could work even if you don't read any other part of the book. What came before was not a way of filling pages, but a way of preparing you for magick. If you are prepared, you can begin.

If you are working on the day of the angel, which is optional, you can begin at any time on that day. In magick, it is sometimes said that days run from sunrise to sunrise, or sunset to sunset, rather than according to our clocks, but this magick appears to work with our perception of the days of the week. If you want to work the magick on a Monday, any time on Monday will work. If you can't work on the ideal day, forget about that aspect and move on with full enthusiasm, at a time of day that works well for you.

You will need somewhere you can be alone to perform the ritual. Privacy is an issue for some, and it is worth putting in the effort to be alone, so you can relax without worrying that somebody will walk in on you. Fortunately, you are not going to be standing in a magick circle, surrounded by candles while burning incense. This does not mean, however, that you should perform the ritual while sitting in a room where people are watching TV, hoping that nobody will notice. You need more mental space than that, to feel and experience the ritual.

I recommend speaking the names and the Sensory Triggers in the ritual. Saying them out loud, and speaking your request, feels magickal, and will often make you sense the angel's presence. If you cannot speak out loud, imagine the words in your mind, and that can be good enough to get results. But if you can find the time to speak the words, do so.

Put in some time before the ritual to word your request. I'll give an example in the ritual, shortly, but you should prepare this in advance. Know what you want, know that this angel can provide a solution, and write a clear request. Learn to pronounce the names. This should only take a few minutes and can all be done days before, or just minutes before the ritual. When you are ready, you may like to work in a dimly lit room or at midday on a balcony in the sunshine. There is no time that works best, in my experience. Some people say they prefer to work after dark when the stars are visible, but I have found the magick works at any time.

To begin, look at the seal of the angel you have chosen. You do not need to understand what is written there, although by now, you will know that the outer ring contains divine names and the name of the ruling archangel. You will also know that the angel's name is written three times, in a celestial alphabet, as a sigil, and in Hebrew. This image seals your connection to the angel, so glance at it for a moment, not thinking about your result, but letting yourself think about the angel's name. Just 'hear' the angel's name in your mind.

As you gaze at the seal in this way, its power is drawn within you, and a connection to the angel is primed. It has not yet been confirmed and established, but it has been readied. You are ready to proceed.

Take a moment to remember that the angels are on your side while you think about what you need. Angels don't need to be convinced, tricked, forced, or commanded. Ask them, and they will help. Continue to gaze at the seal as you contemplate this thought, and know it is true before you continue. (It's ok to look at these instructions at any time, although you will probably learn the ritual quickly, and soon you won't need written instructions.)

When you feel ready, you can begin to chant the first line that appears below the seal. This will always be ELL, EE-AH-OH-EH. Although these are names of God, it is most effective if you begin the chant by saying the names only as sounds. You focus on yourself and your ability to make these sounds. You will find that as you do this, you begin to sense the power of the names. You feel the energy of this chant growing. (Chanting doesn't mean you have to be loud or energetic; you merely say the phrase over and over again.)

If you don't feel much, or if you don't feel anything, don't keep chanting in the hope that you can force something to happen, but accept that you have done the right thing, by opening the ritual, and now move on.

All the protection you need comes from the names you say, and this is more than enough. You are using these names, and an angelic seal, which means there is no danger that an unwanted spirit could interfere. The ritual protects you from unwanted spirits and makes you completely safe.

You now speak the remaining words that are listed below the seal. Remember that after Agla (pronounced as AG-AH-LA), the next line you speak is the name of the ruling archangel. It is important to know this when you say the name. That way, it feels that you are calling for the authority of that archangel to ensure the power of the chosen angel is granted. You don't need to be obsessive, just aware that you are saying the archangel's name. The last word is the name of the angel, and you repeat it three times.

You now speak the Sensory Triggers. If you prefer to read them silently, you can. You may get a strong image, or you may see nothing. This does not matter, as the images are being recognized by your subconscious, and with the angel on the edge of your presence, these triggers bring that connection to completion. Some of these contain the word 'my' so that *you* experience the trigger. For example, you might read, 'A cool hand on my forehead.' This may look strange on the page, but in the context of the ritual, it makes sense, as you are the one experiencing this imagined sensation. You do not need to meditate on these images or think about them for long. Read or say the words, and notice any images that occur to you, and then move on. If you see nothing, that is fine. You may feel the angel's presence when you read the Sensory Triggers.

To complete the connection, say the angel's name again, three times. When that is done, the angel is present and aware of you.

You may sense changes in the way you feel, or the way the room you are in feels. You may sense a strong presence, or feel nothing at all. If you do feel something, allow it to be there, and do not be afraid because it cannot be harmful. If you don't feel anything, avoid disappointment. It is the worst possible emotion to feel during a ritual. Instead, be completely accepting of the fact that you have reached out to the angel, and know that feeling its presence is not a requirement for effective magick.

You now speak your request to the angel. You can read from something you prepared earlier, or speak directly, but keep it short and to the point, as described earlier.

When you have spoken your request, feel gratitude for the help the angel will bring. If you have trouble feeling gratitude, just imagine that what you wish for has already happened. That feels good, so allow yourself to feel good, and feel an inner thanks toward the angel.

In many modern rituals you are urged to perform a mental trick known as 'emotional transmutation,' where you feel the negative energies of the problem or challenge you face, and then transform them to positive energies. Although this works, it is not the best way to work with The Angels of Fortune. Instead, you only need to feel grateful for the angelic intervention. Focus on the result you want, trust that it really will happen, and feel grateful. This step, which sounds so easy, and which *is* so easy, makes the difference between failure and success. The power of gratitude is proven in science and magick, and when the ritual is complete, remembering how grateful you are for angelic intervention, several times a day, can help to make the result manifest. Don't set an alarm to remind yourself, but if you remember the magick or the result you are seeking, feel gratitude for the angel's help. This banishes worry and stress, making the result more likely to come to you.

During the ritual, when you have felt that moment of gratitude, you close the ritual by repeating the first line, ELL, EE-AH-OH-EH, just once. It should feel quite different this time, as though you are ending the magick and returning to your normal life.

You may want to write about your ritual in a magick journal, but as soon as that is done, return to your ordinary life. Lingering in a magickal state does not help as much as returning to your normal life. I prefer to have a sensory experience than to put on the TV, so I find the often recommended advice to cook and eat, or to drink something delicious, is the best advice. Or you can chat with your partner or friends, or go out for a walk. But do not sit and think about the ritual or how it will work, or when it will work. Those energies dampen and blemish the magick.

If you are only performing the ritual for one day, that is all you need to do, and now you can trust and believe that change will come to you. It may not always be as expansive or as slight as you expect. Magick has the potential to disappoint or to exceed all expectations. Remain open to all possibilities and know that when you remain grateful for the presence of the angels, they will begin to respond to your desires.

The Ritual Summary

A summary can be useful when you already understand the instructions.

Before the ritual, write down your request as described.

Begin your ritual in a quiet place where you won't be disturbed.

Look at the seal of the angel you have chosen and 'hear' the angel's name in your mind. Your connection is now primed.

Know that the angels are always on your side. Gaze at the seal and know that this angel will help you.

Chant: ELL, EE-AH-OH-EH. Focus on the sound of the names, and let the energy build. After a short while, or when you feel the time is right, move on.

Speak the remaining words that are listed below the seal. Remember that the last two names are the ruling archangel and the angel. You say the angel's name three times.

Read The Sensory Triggers aloud, and if you see images, enjoy them. If not, don't worry.

To complete the connection, say the angel's name again, three times. The angel is present and aware of you.

Speak your request to the angel, in the form of a statement about what you want and why, as described earlier. Feel gratitude for all the help the angel will bring.

Close the ritual by saying: ELL, EE-AH-OH-EH once, and return to normal life.

The Thirty-Six Angels

On the pages that follow you get everything you need to work with The Angels of Fortune, traditionally known as The Angels of The Decans. The earlier chapters give you the background techniques you need, and if you have any problems with pronunciation, there's a guide at the end of the book.

On the first page, I list the astrological details. These are followed by the ideal day for calling the angel, which is listed as an optional extra.

I then emphasize the pronunciation of the ruling archangel and the angel itself. Below that, you get a description of all the angel's powers, and to make the most of these you will need to understand the earlier chapters.

You then get the seal of the angel, which is used as described in The Ritual of Fortune. You don't need to copy it or print it out. It can be used in the book.

The required Sensory Triggers are listed underneath the seal.

I also list all the divine names beneath each seal, so they are always there when you perform a ritual. The divine names end with Agla (AG-AH-LAH), and the list is completed with the name of the ruling archangel, and finally the angel's name itself.

The descriptions of the powers are short, but they can change your world. Imagine how they can affect you, and they will be able to do so when illuminated with the power of ritual.

1. The Angel Zazer

Zazer is the Angel of the First Decan of Aries.

The Astrological Correspondence is Mars in Aries.

The day of Zazer is Tuesday.

The Ruling Archangel is Malchidiel.

Malchidiel is pronounced as
MAH-LEH-KEY-DEE-ELL

Zazer is pronounced as
ZAH-ZER

Zazer is an angel of achievement and the energy of change. Ask for help from Zazer when you wish to find the energy, courage, or competitive drive to achieve more. This can be useful when starting out on a project, or to renew enthusiasm when it's starting to fade.

You can also ask the angel when you want to make an expected change much smoother. If a relationship is ending, a job is changing, or if you are moving to a new home, these are all the sort of significant changes that could be improved by the support of the angel.

The Seal of Zazer

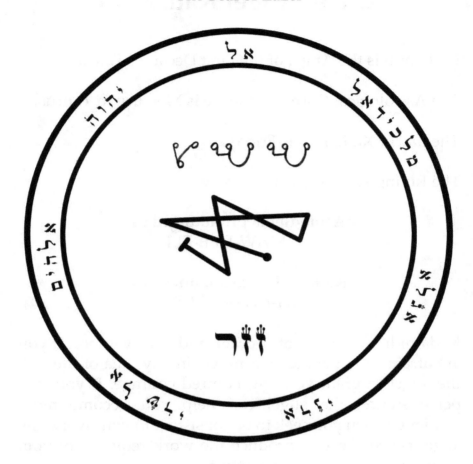

The Sensory Triggers
A red-flamed, white-hot sword.
A towering stone wall where pink roses grow.

ELL, EE-AH-OH-EH
ELL-OH-HEEM
ELL-SHAD-EYE
ADD-OH-NIGH
AG-AH-LAH
MAH-LEH-KEY-DEE-ELL
ZAH-ZER

2. The Angel Kadamidi

Kadamidi is the Angel of the First Decan of Taurus.

The Astrological Correspondence is Mercury in Taurus.

The day of Kadamidi is Friday.

The Ruling Archangel is Asmodiel.

Asmodiel is pronounced as
AZ-MAW-DEE-ELL

Kadamidi is pronounced as
KAH-DAM-EE-DEE

Kadamidi is an angel of courage and perseverance. If you are afraid to make the next move, in any area of life, ask the angel to grant you the required courage. If you lack perseverance, the angel can help you become more resilient. When you seek to be consistent in your work, the angel can make you produce the work required of you, regularly, and with far less effort.

The angel can also improve your business acumen, especially when it comes to negotiating with others.

The angel's connection to consistency also means it can affect your ability to overcome stubborn habits. If you have any bad habits, unwanted traits, or ways of being that don't fit in with who you want to be, ask the angel to release you from their bond.

The Seal of Kadamidi

The Sensory Triggers
Green shoots in the dark, wet earth.
The deep red of sunset.

ELL, EE-AH-OH-EH
ELL-OH-HEEM
ELL-SHAD-EYE
ADD-OH-NIGH
AG-AH-LAH
AZ-MAW-DEE-ELL
KAH-DAM-EE-DEE

3. The Angel Sagarash

Sagarash is the Angel of the First Decan of Gemini.

The Astrological Correspondence is Jupiter in Gemini.

The day of Sagarash is Wednesday.

The Ruling Archangel is Ambriel.

Ambriel is pronounced as
AM-BREE-ELL

Sagarash is pronounced as
SAG-AH-RASH

Sagarash is an angel of curiosity and wonder. If you have grown disillusioned with the world, ask the angel to renew your sense of wonder, helping you find what it is that you are still curious about. People who believe they know everything do not thrive as well as those who are curious. It is an underestimated power that has helped many of the greatest inventors and leaders to their finest achievements.

The Seal of Sagarash

The Sensory Triggers
A white horse on a green hilltop.
An orange sunset.

ELL, EE-AH-OH-EH
ELL-OH-HEEM
ELL-SHAD-EYE
ADD-OH-NIGH
AG-AH-LAH
AM-BREE-ELL
SAG-AH-RASH

4. The Angel Mathravash

Mathravash is the Angel of the First Decan of Cancer.

The Astrological Correspondence is Venus in Cancer.

The day of Mathravash is Monday.

The Ruling Archangel is Muriel.

Muriel is pronounced as
MOO-REE-ELL

Mathravash is pronounced as
MATH-RAH-VASH

Mathravash can help you to get through the most difficult times, while remaining calm and compassionate. This can be helpful when there are complex family problems, unexpected accidents, or other events that bring pressure and a feeling of panic. With this power, you become the person that people will turn to, and you will feel willing and able to guide everybody to happier times.

The angel is also strong with the power of acceptance. If you are having difficulty accepting responsibility for something, the angel can assist you. If somebody else cannot accept something you have done, you can ask the angel to urge that person to be more understanding.

The Seal of Mathravash

The Sensory Triggers
Green ivy covering a white marble statue of a man.
A field of sunflowers.

ELL, EE-AH-OH-EH
ELL-OH-HEEM
ELL-SHAD-EYE
ADD-OH-NIGH
AG-AH-LAH
MOO-REE-ELL
MATH-RAH-VASH

5. The Angel Losanahar

Losanahar is the Angel of the First Decan of Leo.

The Astrological Correspondence is Saturn in Leo.

The day of Losanahar is Sunday.

The Ruling Archangel is Verachiel.

Verachiel is pronounced as
VEH-RAH-KEY-ELL

Losanahar is pronounced as
LAW-SAN-AH-HAR

Losanahar can encourage others to believe in your abilities, support your ambitions, and even invest in your dreams.

If you are filled with ambitious energy but haven't yet worked out the best way to use that energy, ask the angel for guidance. You will discover the smartest ways to work.

Losanahar is also an angel of passionate lust. If you have a strong desire to be with somebody, you can ask the angel to let the other person sense what you are feeling. This doesn't seduce the other person but can stir latent feelings and improve the possibility of a connection.

The Seal of Losanahar

The Sensory Triggers
A red-leafed tree against a dark, stormy sky.
Yellow flames.

ELL, EE-AH-OH-EH
ELL-OH-HEEM
ELL-SHAD-EYE
ADD-OH-NIGH
AG-AH-LAH
VEH-RAH-KEY-ELL
LAW-SAN-AH-HAR

6. The Angel Ananaurah

Ananaurah is the Angel of the First Decan of Virgo.

The Astrological Correspondence is The Sun in Virgo.

The day of Ananaurah is Wednesday.

The Ruling Archangel is Hamaliel.

Hamaliel is pronounced as
HAH-MAH-LEE-ELL

Ananaurah is pronounced as
AN-AN-AH-OO-RAH

Ananaurah is an angel of intimacy and can help any relationship become closer and warmer.

The angel can also help you to attain deep relaxation. If you use a regular practice, such as meditation, ask the angel to support this and you will achieve deep states of relaxation. If you struggle to sleep, the angel can help bring a calm that induces sleep.

If your home or work environment feels too chaotic, through your actions or those of people around you, ask Ananaurah to bring calm and order.

The Seal of Ananaurah

The Sensory Triggers
A shattered pomegranate on white marble.
A large stone crowned with green moss.

ELL, EE-AH-OH-EH
ELL-OH-HEEM
ELL-SHAD-EYE
ADD-OH-NIGH
AG-AH-LAH
HAH-MAH-LEE-ELL
AN-AN-AH-OO-RAH

7. The Angel Tarasni

Tarasni is the Angel of the First Decan of Libra.

The Astrological Correspondence is The Moon in Libra.

The day of Tarasni is Friday.

The Ruling Archangel is Zuriel.

Zuriel is pronounced as
ZOO-REE-ELL

Tarasni is pronounced as
TAH-RAZ-NEE

Tarasni is an angel of harmony who can heal damaged relationships. When you want to restore a friendship or relationship, the angel can help. If a relationship is over the angel cannot force somebody to love you again, but if needless arguments have caused damage, you may restore peace and regain trust. In other cases, you may be able to remain friends after a breakup. Damaged friendships are sometimes more difficult to heal, but the angel will support your efforts to reconcile.

When you need to tell somebody some difficult news, ask the angel to bring understanding. This will make you calmer and can help the other person to hear what you are really trying to say, instead of jumping to conclusions.

The Seal of Tarasni

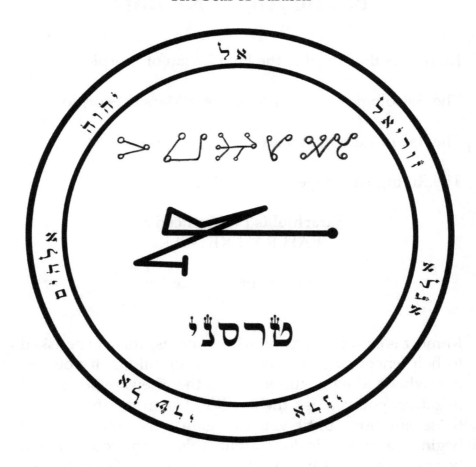

The Sensory Triggers
A burning branch on hard earth.
Green seaweed in the sunlit ocean.

ELL, EE-AH-OH-EH
ELL-OH-HEEM
ELL-SHAD-EYE
ADD-OH-NIGH
AG-AH-LAH
ZOO-REE-ELL
TAH-RAZ-NEE

8. The Angel Kamotz

Kamotz is the Angel of the First Decan of Scorpio.

The Astrological Correspondence is Mars in Scorpio.

The day of Kamotz is Tuesday.

The Ruling Archangel is Barachiel.

Barachiel is pronounced as
BAH-RAH-KEY-ELL

Kamotz is pronounced as
CAM-ORTS

Kamotz is connected to intense emotions, and can be asked to help encourage or subdue these emotions. If you feel overwhelmed with emotions, whether they are positive or negative, you can ask the angel to lessen the intensity of those emotions until you can gain perspective. At the beginning of a wild love affair, this might sound like a boring choice, but it could be one you are glad you have made. The opposite power is also available, and you can ask the angel to attract passionate relationships into your life. How well this works depends on how often you meet people and how willing you are to put yourself out there, but if you do, without actually seeking passion too obsessively, then passion can find you.

Kamotz is also an angel of secrecy, and if you have something you need to hide, the angel will help you keep knowledge hidden.

The Seal of Kamotz

The Sensory Triggers
A dagger with a blade of sharp, white stone.
A green river between two snowy mountains.

ELL, EE-AH-OH-EH
ELL-OH-HEEM
ELL-SHAD-EYE
ADD-OH-NIGH
AG-AH-LAH
BAH-RAH-KEY-ELL
CAM-ORTS

9. The Angel Mishrath

Mishrath is the Angel of the First Decan of Sagittarius.

The Astrological Correspondence is Mercury in Sagittarius.

The day of Mishrath is Thursday.

The Ruling Archangel is Advachiel.

Advachiel is pronounced as
ADD-VAH-KEY-ELL

Mishrath is pronounced as
MEESH-RATH

Mishrath can make you able to achieve more in less time. This is a powerful magick that seems to bend time itself so that you are able to make good plans and achieve everything you need to. If a deadline is upon you, when time is running out, or if you want to take on a large project when time is limited, the angel can make it possible. On a more everyday level, it can be used by anybody who feels time-poor, to find a few extra hours in the week to pursue a beloved hobby or any other important activity.

Mishrath can support your efforts to be honest if you need to tell somebody a difficult truth. The angel is also able to give you a feeling of optimism when you are filled with doubt. The optimism will never be unrealistic but will let you sense the genuine potential of the life that awaits you.

The Seal of Mishrath

The Sensory Triggers
A garden of red and white flowers.
A black boulder at the ocean's edge.

ELL, EE-AH-OH-EH
ELL-OH-HEEM
ELL-SHAD-EYE
ADD-OH-NIGH
AG-AH-LAH
ADD-VAH-KEY-ELL
MEESH-RATH

10. The Angel Misnin

Misnin is the Angel of the First Decan of Capricorn.

The Astrological Correspondence is Jupiter in Capricorn.

The day of Misnin is Saturday.

The Ruling Archangel is Haniel.

Haniel is pronounced as
HAH-NEE-ELL

Misnin is pronounced as
ME-SAH-NEEN

Misnin is an angel of ambition and can help you find and achieve your ambitions. If you are in the early stages of finding out what it is you want from life, ask the angel to guide you to the sights, sounds, thoughts, people, and places that will inspire your journey. If your ambitions are already clear, ask the angel to give you guidance regarding how to achieve them and the next steps to take. If you are close to achieving an ambition, ask the angel to support a crucial moment in your progress.

Misnin can help you maximize your intelligence, especially with regards to your hopes and dreams. If you need to learn something new, pass an exam, or achieve anything that requires brain-power, ask the angel to help you connect with the true potential of your innate intelligence.

The Seal of Misnin

The Sensory Triggers
A lake of blue-white ice.
Dark blue flowers growing through the snow.

ELL, EE-AH-OH-EH
ELL-OH-HEEM
ELL-SHAD-EYE
ADD-OH-NIGH
AG-AH-LAH
HAH-NEE-ELL
ME-SAH-NEEN

11. The Angel Saspam

Saspam is the Angel of the First Decan of Aquarius.

The Astrological Correspondence is Venus in Aquarius.

The day of Saspam is Saturday.

The Ruling Archangel is Cambriel.

Cambriel is pronounced as
CAM-BREE-ELL

Saspam is pronounced as
SAH-SEP-AHM

Saspam can help you find the courage to start over. If your life feels in need of renewal, and you need the courage to let go of old dreams and ambitions, to make way for new ones, the angel can help. You might wonder why anybody would want help to give up on dreams, but this isn't about giving up or giving in. This power is about freedom. When you feel burdened by your dreams, rather than liberated and enthused, you may need to move on, but it takes courage. This angel can help you find that courage.

Saspam can also help you get started on a new project with an enthusiasm that will last. If you are excited about something but worry you won't complete it, Saspam can help you begin something that you will see through to completion. If you want to write a song, record an album, write a novel, or work on any lengthy and demanding project, the angel can help you start in the best way.

The Seal of Saspam

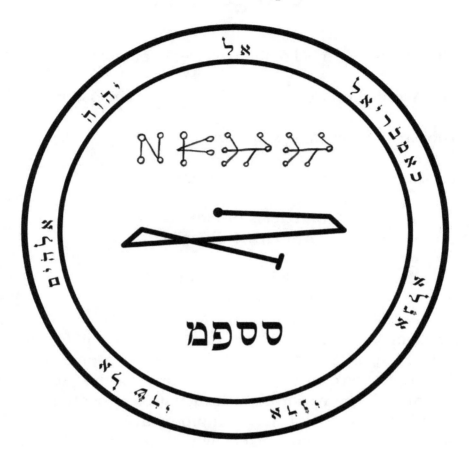

The Sensory Triggers
Red poppies in a green field.
The sun, low over the ocean and deep red.

ELL, EE-AH-OH-EH
ELL-OH-HEEM
ELL-SHAD-EYE
ADD-OH-NIGH
AG-AH-LAH
CAM-BREE-ELL
SAH-SEP-AHM

12. The Angel Bihelami

Bihelami is the Angel of the First Decan of Pisces.

The Astrological Correspondence is Saturn in Pisces.

The day of Bihelami is Monday.

The Ruling Archangel is Amnitziel.

Amnitziel is pronounced as
AM-NEAT-SEE-ELL

Bihelami is pronounced as
BEE-HEH-LAH-ME

Bihelami is an angel of art, and if you want to find inspiration, ask this angel for help. Creative people know that inspiration comes when you create all the time, so give this magick the opportunity to manifest by working at your art, even if it feels unproductive. A flash of inspiration is far more likely when you are willing to commit to your creative work.

If you are ambitious, especially in the arts, it can be difficult to choose the best options to work on, and how to promote and share your work. Any time you need guidance, ask Bihelami for help.

The Seal of Bihelami

The Sensory Triggers
A cool hand on my forehead.
White clouds in a blue sky.

ELL, EE-AH-OH-EH
ELL-OH-HEEM
ELL-SHAD-EYE
ADD-OH-NIGH
AG-AH-LAH
AM-NEAT-SEE-ELL
BEE-HEH-LAH-ME

13. The Angel Behahemi

Behahemi is the Angel of the Second Decan of Aries.

The Astrological Correspondence is The Sun in Aries.

The day of Behahemi is Tuesday.

The Ruling Archangel is Malchidiel.

Malchidiel is pronounced as
MAH-LEH-KEY-DEE-ELL

Behahemi is pronounced as
BEH-HAH-HEM-EE

Behahemi is an angel that can help you be more charismatic. In some situations, charisma is the key to being noticed, understood, admired, and appreciated. The charisma can be energetic and outgoing if that is what you are looking for. If you aren't naturally flamboyant, or if you prefer to be quieter, you can develop a strong and steady charm. Either of these states can be used to make you more attractive and popular, but they can also be used to make you more influential. Many people are more easily convinced by charisma (or cool charm).

If you find that you are obsessing over past mistakes, incidents, relationships, or dreams that died, you can ask Behahemi to help you live in the moment. When you appreciate the present, you attract more enjoyable experiences into your future.

The Seal of Behahemi

The Sensory Triggers
Standing in still, cool water up to my ankles.
The glitter of a frosted field in a white sunrise.

ELL, EE-AH-OH-EH
ELL-OH-HEEM
ELL-SHAD-EYE
ADD-OH-NIGH
AG-AH-LAH
MAH-LEH-KEY-DEE-ELL
BEH-HAH-HEM-EE

14. The Angel Minacharai

Minacharai is the Angel of the Second Decan of Taurus.

The Astrological Correspondence is The Moon in Taurus.

The day of Minacharai is Friday.

The Ruling Archangel is Asmodiel.

Asmodiel is pronounced as
AZ-MAW-DEE-ELL

Minacharai is pronounced as
ME-NAH-CAH-RAH-EE

Minacharai is an angel that helps build ongoing financial security by helping you make the best decisions where money is concerned. If you have drawn a complete blank and don't know how to make money, seek guidance from the angel. If you are doing ok but still feel like poverty could be around the corner, ask the angel to inspire a new way forward. The work is still yours to be done, and money won't appear from nowhere, but a serious commitment to financial security will be rewarded well by Minacharai.

When you require more discipline or perseverance, to pursue an activity that is important to you, yet difficult, ask for help from this angel. When you are trying to lose weight, break a habit, or get fit, this is the angel that can support you.

The Seal of Minacharai

The Sensory Triggers
Pink blossom against a blue sky.
A ring of white gold around my right wrist.

ELL, EE-AH-OH-EH
ELL-OH-HEEM
ELL-SHAD-EYE
ADD-OH-NIGH
AG-AH-LAH
AZ-MAW-DEE-ELL
ME-NAH-CAH-RAH-EE

15. The Angel Shehadani

Shehadani is the Angel of the Second Decan of Gemini.

The Astrological Correspondence is Mars in Gemini.

The day of Shehadani is Wednesday.

The Ruling Archangel is Ambriel.

Ambriel is pronounced as
AM-BREE-ELL

Shehadani is pronounced as
SHEH-HAH-DAH-NEE

Shehadani can help you predict or sense upcoming financial changes. That means that if you work in finance, trading stocks, shares, and similar products, your ability to make predictions will be greatly enhanced. You will need the skills of a good trader to take advantage of this ability.

Shehadani helps you appreciate or discover your gifts. If you feel uninspired, ask the angel to reveal your gifts, and you may be reminded of old hobbies and interests, or discover something new.

The Seal of Shehadani

The Sensory Triggers
A silver crown on a black stone dais.
A warm orange flame.

ELL, EE-AH-OH-EH
ELL-OH-HEEM
ELL-SHAD-EYE
ADD-OH-NIGH
AG-AH-LAH
AM-BREE-ELL
SHEH-HAH-DAH-NEE

16. The Angel Rahadetz

Rahadetz is the Angel of the Second Decan of Cancer.

The Astrological Correspondence is Mercury in Cancer.

The day of Rahadetz is Monday.

The Ruling Archangel is Muriel.

Muriel is pronounced as
MOO-REE-ELL

Rahadetz is pronounced as
RAH-HAH-DETS

Rahadetz helps you achieve the feeling of abundance through the power of intuition. Abundance is the feeling you get when money comes easily, when nothing seems to cost too much, and when all that you need is readily available. In this state, you are not greedy or indulgent, but at ease with all that you have without yearning for more. If you want to feel abundant, the angel can improve your intuition so that you sense opportunities that could increase the abundance in your life. When you experience the feeling of abundance, it is easier to make bold and imaginative plans, without being reckless.

The angel can also help you with feelings of self-respect, allowing you to know what your strengths are, and easing fears, doubts, and guilt.

The Seal of Rahadetz

The Sensory Triggers
A pale-yellow moon in the early evening.
The scent of the ocean.

ELL, EE-AH-OH-EH
ELL-OH-HEEM
ELL-SHAD-EYE
ADD-OH-NIGH
AG-AH-LAH
MOO-REE-ELL
RAH-HAH-DETS

17. The Angel Zachi

Zachi is the Angel of the Second Decan of Leo.

The Astrological Correspondence is Jupiter in Leo.

The day of Zachi is Sunday.

The Ruling Archangel is Verachiel.

Verachiel is pronounced as
VEH-RAH-KEY-ELL

Zachi is pronounced as
ZACK-EH-EE

Zachi is the embodiment of triumph and can help you succeed in many areas. This angel's focus is more about short-term gains than long-term success, but you can use those small successes to build to a much larger success. When you need to triumph in any form of competition, ask the angel for help. You can find success in sports, when trying to land a deal, when you want to be the one chosen for a particular project, and in any other area where you would feel triumphant if it all went well.

The angel can also help you motivate others to work to the best of their ability, especially in creative areas. For leaders of large creative teams, such as film directors, this angel is invaluable.

The Seal of Zachi

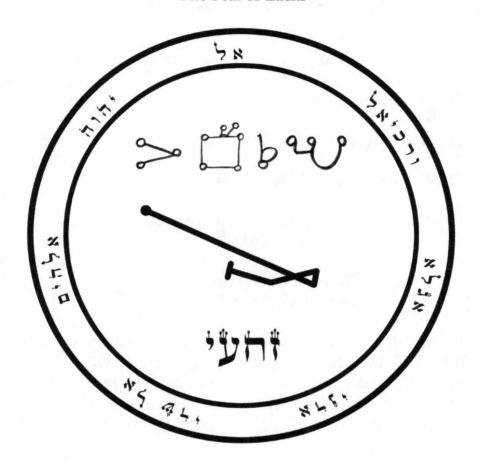

The Sensory Triggers
Summer breeze and yellow wildflowers.
White blossom on a green tree.

ELL, EE-AH-OH-EH
ELL-OH-HEEM
ELL-SHAD-EYE
ADD-OH-NIGH
AG-AH-LAH
VEH-RAH-KEY-ELL
ZACK-EH-EE

18. The Angel Rayadyah

Rayadyah is the Angel of the Second Decan of Virgo.

The Astrological Correspondence is Venus in Virgo.

The day of Rayadyah is Wednesday.

The Ruling Archangel is Hamaliel.

Hamaliel is pronounced as
HAH-MAH-LEE-ELL

Rayadyah is pronounced as
RAY-AH-DEE-AH

Rayadyah can help when you need patience, clear thinking, and the ability to be diplomatic with others. These times don't often occur, for most people, but when they do, this angel can save you from setbacks. The angel is also helpful when you are learning highly technical skills.

The angel can bring good fortune in matters of finance. When you feel you need a stroke of luck in money matters, ask the angel for help. I doubt this will help with gambling but I have seen it bring financial luck in many creative ways. Remember not to focus on the process but the result you desire.

Rayadyah is also powerful at helping you and your partner feel the true depths of passion in a relationship, whether the relationship is old or new.

The Seal of Rayadyah

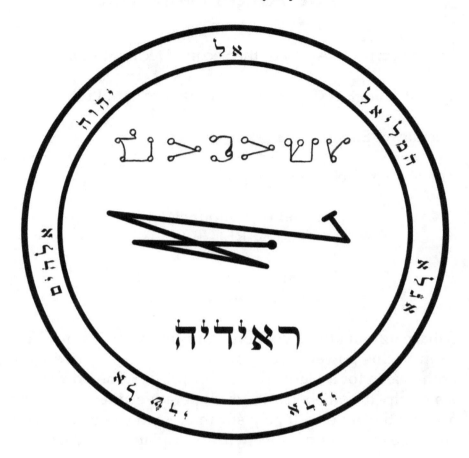

The Sensory Triggers
A black tree with emerald green leaves.
Soft rain on a grassy hillside.

ELL, EE-AH-OH-EH
ELL-OH-HEEM
ELL-SHAD-EYE
ADD-OH-NIGH
AG-AH-LAH
HAH-MAH-LEE-ELL
RAY-AH-DEE-AH

19. The Angel Saharnatz

Saharnatz is the Angel of the Second Decan of Libra.

The Astrological Correspondence is Saturn in Libra.

The day of Saharnatz is Friday.

The Ruling Archangel is Zuriel.

Zuriel is pronounced as
ZOO-REE-ELL

Saharnatz is pronounced as
SAH-HAR-NAHTS

Saharnatz can attract cooperation from other people. You can use this power when you want people to share your enthusiasm for a planned event or project. The power can also help if somebody is uncooperative due to fear or apathy; the angel will help stir interest in somebody who could be more cooperative with your plans and ideas.

You can also achieve a feeling of justice with Saharnatz. Ask the angel to help in any situation where you feel you have been wronged, or when you are facing a legal challenge. The angel is extremely powerful at bringing a good solution in these situations.

The Seal of Saharnatz

The Sensory Triggers
Moss on the trunk of a wide, black tree.
Frost on fallen autumn leaves.

ELL, EE-AH-OH-EH
ELL-OH-HEEM
ELL-SHAD-EYE
ADD-OH-NIGH
AG-AH-LAH
ZOO-REE-ELL
SAH-HAR-NAHTS

20. The Angel Nundohar

Nundohar is the Angel of the Second Decan of Scorpio.

The Astrological Correspondence is The Sun in Scorpio.

The day of Nundohar is Tuesday.

The Ruling Archangel is Barachiel.

Barachiel is pronounced as
BAH-RAH-KEY-ELL

Nundohar is pronounced as
NUN-DAW-HAR

Nundohar can make others see you as more trustworthy. The angel won't deceive others, but if you are a trustworthy person, and need to be seen that way by many people, or one specific person, the angel can help your honesty to shine.

An important aspect of Nundohar is a sense of integrity. If you ever find that your work, your art, or your relationships lack the integrity that you want them to have, the angel will bring transformation. This can help if ever you feel like a fraud, a sell-out, or just that you're not being completely true to yourself.

The Seal of Nundohar

The Sensory Triggers
An apple tree, laden with green apples.
A handful of red soil.

ELL, EE-AH-OH-EH
ELL-OH-HEEM
ELL-SHAD-EYE
ADD-OH-NIGH
AG-AH-LAH
BAH-RAH-KEY-ELL
NUN-DAW-HAR

21. The Angel Vehrin

Vehrin is the Angel of the Second Decan of Sagittarius.

The Astrological Correspondence is The Moon in Sagittarius.

The day of Vehrin is Thursday.

The Ruling Archangel is Advachiel.

Advachiel is pronounced as
ADD-VAH-KEY-ELL

Vehrin is pronounced as
VEH-REEN

Vehrin is powerful with the energy of independence. You can use this power to think independently when others are trying to influence you. If you feel you are being influenced by friends, thought patterns, old 'messages' ingrained from your upbringing, or even by the influence of dark magick, ask the angel to free your thoughts, so they are your own. The revelations that can occur when your mind is set free can be life-changing.

If you are going traveling, ask that angel to make you able to enjoy the trip without expectations. Often, travel plans are ruined by set expectations which can rarely be met, but with the support of this angel, you can let go of expectations and enjoy the experience, even when things don't go according to plan.

The Seal of Vehrin

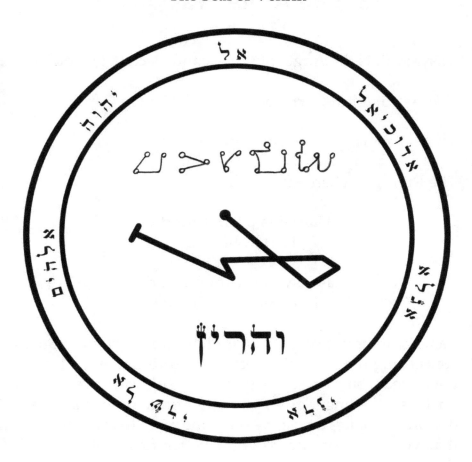

The Sensory Triggers
A warm breeze with the scent of soil.
A strong wind pulls red leaves from trees.

ELL, EE-AH-OH-EH
ELL-OH-HEEM
ELL-SHAD-EYE
ADD-OH-NIGH
AG-AH-LAH
ADD-VAH-KEY-ELL
VEH-REEN

22. The Angel Yasyasyah

Yasyasyah is the Angel of the Second Decan of Capricorn.

The Astrological Correspondence is Mars in Capricorn.

The day of Yasyasyah is Saturday.

The Ruling Archangel is Haniel.

Haniel is pronounced as
HAH-NEE-ELL

Yasyasyah is pronounced as
EE-AS-EE-AS-EE-AH

Yasyasyah gives you strong determination in matters concerning money. Whether you're trying to get a loan, a good deal, buy or sell a house, or seeking investors in business, the angel gives you a determination that opens doors and makes a positive outcome more likely. Any time that you are working to get a better financial deal, the angel can help.

The angel can give you a similar style of determination in your chosen career, helping you commit to the hard work necessary for success, and causing that hard work to pay off more often.

If you find that somebody in your life is too stubborn, this angel can help to make them more willing to hear your side of the story.

The Seal of Yasyasyah

The Sensory Triggers
Icicles hang from the branches of a tree.
A rocky waterfall, white with misty spray.

ELL, EE-AH-OH-EH
ELL-OH-HEEM
ELL-SHAD-EYE
ADD-OH-NIGH
AG-AH-LAH
HAH-NEE-ELL
EE-AS-EE-AS-EE-AH

23. The Angel Abdaron

Abdaron is the Angel of the Second Decan of Aquarius.

The Astrological Correspondence is Mercury in Aquarius.

The day of Abdaron is Saturday.

The Ruling Archangel is Cambriel.

Cambriel is pronounced as
CAM-BREE-ELL

Abdaron is pronounced as
AB-DAH-RAWN

Abdaron can improve your visual skills by helping you to perceive more clearly. This can improve all forms of art, and can also support your efforts to visualize. If you use your imagination in work, magick, or art, your imagination can be empowered by the angel improving your perception (which is the source of all imagination).

The angel can also help you to see the truth of a situation by extending your ability to perceive what other people are thinking, planning, and feeling. If there is a situation that concerns and affects you, seek a deeper perception, and the angel will help you understand what is occurring.

The Seal of Abdaron

The Sensory Triggers
Violet flowers growing through the snow.
A still pond reflecting the white sky.

ELL, EE-AH-OH-EH
ELL-OH-HEEM
ELL-SHAD-EYE
ADD-OH-NIGH
AG-AH-LAH
CAM-BREE-ELL
AB-DAH-RAWN

24. The Angel Avron

Avron is the Angel of the Second Decan of Pisces.

The Astrological Correspondence is Jupiter in Pisces.

The day of Avron is Monday.

The Ruling Archangel is Amnitziel.

Amnitziel is pronounced as
AM-NEAT-SEE-ELL

Avron is pronounced as
AV-RAWN

Avron can bring relief when you know something is bothering or upsetting you, but you are unable to release the feelings. If you feel confused about why your mood is low, or why you are unhappy or lacking direction, the angel will bring you clarity and relief and can help you see a way out of the situation. At times when you feel at a loss, uncertain, or dismayed by life, this can be enormously empowering.

If you want to develop your intuition, this angel can help. It can also improve your ability to read meaning in signs and omens, and can improve any form of divination that you use.

The Seal of Avron

The Sensory Triggers
A lake, the ice frozen like clear glass.
A frosted field in a red sunrise.

ELL, EE-AH-OH-EH
ELL-OH-HEEM
ELL-SHAD-EYE
ADD-OH-NIGH
AG-AH-LAH
AM-NEAT-SEE-ELL
AV-RAWN

25. The Angel Satonder

Satonder is the Angel of the Third Decan of Aries.

The Astrological Correspondence is Venus in Aries.

The day of Satonder is Tuesday.

The Ruling Archangel is Malchidiel.

Malchidiel is pronounced as
MAH-LEH-KEY-DEE-ELL

Satonder is pronounced as
SAH-TAWN-DER

Satonder is an angel who is strong with the powers of finance. If you want to turn your attention to making more money, you can ask the angel for guidance, finding the best way to make more money from your current position. You can also request more money for specific needs, although you should not specify how you will receive that money. If you want to become more financially secure, or move into a different level of earnings, or seek support for a business venture that could reap rewards, the angel will make all financial aspects more likely to work in your favor.

If you want to be commercially successful, the angel will support your efforts to build the income you need from your work.

The Seal of Satonder

The Sensory Triggers
Golden sunrise over dark mountains.
Red berries on a leafless tree.

ELL, EE-AH-OH-EH
ELL-OH-HEEM
ELL-SHAD-EYE
ADD-OH-NIGH
AG-AH-LAH
MAH-LEH-KEY-DEE-ELL
SAH-TAWN-DER

26. The Angel Yakasaganotz

Yakasaganotz is the Angel of the Third Decan of Taurus.

The Astrological Correspondence is Saturn in Taurus.

The day of Yakasaganotz is Friday.

The Ruling Archangel is Asmodiel.

Asmodiel is pronounced as
AZ-MAW-DEE-ELL

Yakasaganotz is pronounced as
YAH-KAH-SAH-GAH-NAUGHTS

Yakasaganotz is useful for opening up new roads or pathways through life. If you know there is a blockage preventing you from moving forward, whether it's a mental, emotional, or spiritual blockage, the angel can help you move forward. If you are looking for a new way to live, with a complete overhaul of your purpose, seek guidance from this angel.

Yakasaganotz is also a highly practical angel in matters of finance and can help when you are making plans to save or invest your money. Good decisions made early make a big difference to your life, and if you are in a position to save or invest your money, you will find the wisdom you need from this angel.

The Seal of Yakasaganotz

The Sensory Triggers
A pink seashell where the waves break.
A tiny stream that trickles through the forest.

ELL, EE-AH-OH-EH
ELL-OH-HEEM
ELL-SHAD-EYE
ADD-OH-NIGH
AG-AH-LAH
AZ-MAW-DEE-ELL
YAH-KAH-SAH-GAH-NAUGHTS

27. The Angel Bethon

Bethon is the Angel of the Third Decan of Gemini.

The Astrological Correspondence is The Sun in Gemini.

The day of Bethon is Wednesday.

The Ruling Archangel is Ambriel.

Ambriel is pronounced as
AM-BREE-ELL

Bethon is pronounced as
BEE-THORN

Bethon is the angel you turn to when you need to write well. The angel will improve your confidence about what you have to see, and your skills with the written word.

If you are a public speaker or actor, the angel can help you to speak and express yourself and can help you recall the required words easily, without the need for notes.

Bethon is also an angel of friendship and makes new connections possible by giving you more confidence, without you feeling the need to inflate your ego and prove yourself. This makes you more likable. If you are seeking new friends or trying to cement a new friendship, ask the angel for help.

The Seal of Bethon

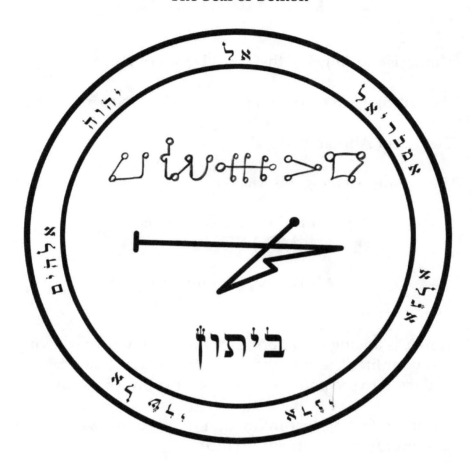

The Sensory Triggers
Oranges grow on leafy trees.
A cool breeze as the sky darkens.

ELL, EE-AH-OH-EH
ELL-OH-HEEM
ELL-SHAD-EYE
ADD-OH-NIGH
AG-AH-LAH
AM-BREE-ELL
BEE-THORN

28. The Angel Alinkir

Alinkir is the Angel of the Third Decan of Cancer.

The Astrological Correspondence is The Moon in Cancer.

The day of Alinkir is Monday.

The Ruling Archangel is Muriel.

Muriel is pronounced as
MOO-REE-ELL

Alinkir is pronounced as
AH-LEEN-KEER

Alinkir is an angel that brings relief when worry is taking over your life. The angel can ease the feelings of worry and guide you to see potential solutions to your problems.

If you are feeling lost in life and don't know what to do next, the angel can offer guidance.

Alinkir can help reconnect you with loved ones in a meaningful way. If you feel there has been damage or withdrawal in a relationship of any kind, you can ask for the angel to reconnect you to somebody. It can be a moving and rewarding experience when you feel that happen. The angel will influence the other person to be warmer and more open to you, while making you warmer and more open to them.

The Seal of Alinkir

The Sensory Triggers
A blue egg in its brown nest.
Red leaves fall into green grass.

ELL, EE-AH-OH-EH
ELL-OH-HEEM
ELL-SHAD-EYE
ADD-OH-NIGH
AG-AH-LAH
MOO-REE-ELL
AH-LEEN-KEER

29. The Angel Sahiber

Sahiber is the Angel of the Third Decan of Leo.

The Astrological Correspondence is Mars in Leo.

The day of Sahiber is Sunday.

The Ruling Archangel is Verachiel.

Verachiel is pronounced as
VEH-RAH-KEY-ELL

Sahiber is pronounced as
SAH-EE-BEAR

Sahiber can give you the willpower to reach a goal. If you are trying to take one more step toward a major goal, you can ask the angel to help you make that step. You can also ask the angel to oversee your willpower all the way to that final goal, even if it is a year away.

If you are looking to develop your leadership qualities, the angel can help. It won't make you appear more like a leader than you are, but will work on your actual abilities to lead others well.

This is also an angel of kindness, and you can ask the angel to grant mercy and comfort to somebody you know who is suffering.

The Seal of Sahiber

The Sensory Triggers
My feet in cool mud at the riverside.
A yellow fire crackles.

ELL, EE-AH-OH-EH
ELL-OH-HEEM
ELL-SHAD-EYE
ADD-OH-NIGH
AG-AH-LAH
VEH-RAH-KEY-ELL
SAH-EE-BEAR

30. The Angel Mishpar

Mishpar is the Angel of the Third Decan of Virgo.

The Astrological Correspondence is Mercury in Virgo.

The day of Mishpar is Wednesday.

The Ruling Archangel is Hamaliel.

Hamaliel is pronounced as
HAH-MAH-LEE-ELL

Mishpar is pronounced as
MEESH-PAR

Mishpar is useful for good planning and decision-making. This is backed up by good observation and reasoning. Magickal powers can be made to sound more exciting if they are described in exciting ways, but this power is something you should get excited about even though it sounds less exciting than others. Many people want to do something about their career, or their creative work, or another important part of life, and making good plans and decisions is what it takes. That makes this one of the greatest powers.

If you need to spend more time planning while using good observation to see what others are doing, the angel can help with your powers of observation. In a competitive environment, observation and planning are invaluable.

You can also ask the angel to give you more purpose and energy, when you are working on something, or when you lack direction and don't even know what your purpose might be.

The Seal of Mishpar

The Sensory Triggers
Green leaves fall on green grass.
Warm air on a starry night.

ELL, EE-AH-OH-EH
ELL-OH-HEEM
ELL-SHAD-EYE
ADD-OH-NIGH
AG-AH-LAH
HAH-MAH-LEE-ELL
MEESH-PAR

31. The Angel Shachdar

Shachdar is the Angel of the Third Decan of Libra.

The Astrological Correspondence is Jupiter in Libra.

The day of Shachdar is Friday.

The Ruling Archangel is Zuriel.

Zuriel is pronounced as
ZOO-REE-ELL

Shachdar is pronounced as
SHAH-KAH-DAR

Shachdar is strong with the powers of harmony and balance, and can restore a sense of order and stability when your life has tumbled out of control, or when other people have become a destabilizing factor. The power can be used to bring balance to homes, relationships, workplaces, and even neighborhoods.

The angel can repel evil, and often does so by attracting more love and warmth into your life. If you know there is evil directed at you, either through magick or through ordinary means, Shachdar can protect you, even if you don't know the source of the evil. If you feel like your life has become lonely or disconnected from people, you can ask for more loving warmth from those you know, as well as the potential to meet new people who will bring love and warmth.

The Seal of Shachdar

The Sensory Triggers
Pale pink flowers in dry grass.
A dagger with a silver blade.

ELL, EE-AH-OH-EH
ELL-OH-HEEM
ELL-SHAD-EYE
ADD-OH-NIGH
AG-AH-LAH
ZOO-REE-ELL
SHAH-KAH-DAR

32. The Angel Uthrodiel

Uthrodiel is the Angel of the Third Decan of Scorpio.

The Astrological Correspondence is Venus in Scorpio.

The day of Uthrodiel is Tuesday.

The Ruling Archangel is Barachiel.

Barachiel is pronounced as
BAH-RAH-KEY-ELL

Uthrodiel is pronounced as
OO-THRAW-DEE-ELL

Uthrodiel is an angel that understands the changing desires and needs you have about your career. If you are looking for a new career, or a shift in your career plans, ask this angel for guidance.

Uthrodiel has a strong connection to money. If you are looking for a promotion, raising money for a business project, or seeking more money for a specific project or activity, you will gain support from this angel.

The Seal of Uthrodiel

The Sensory Triggers
A white tree against dark clouds.
Heavy rain on a rushing river.

ELL, EE-AH-OH-EH
ELL-OH-HEEM
ELL-SHAD-EYE
ADD-OH-NIGH
AG-AH-LAH
BAH-RAH-KEY-ELL
OO-THRAW-DEE-ELL

33. The Angel Aboha

Aboha is the Angel of the Third Decan of Sagittarius.

The Astrological Correspondence is Saturn in Sagittarius.

The day of Aboha is Thursday.

The Ruling Archangel is Advachiel.

Advachiel is pronounced as
ADD-VAH-KEY-ELL

Aboha is pronounced as
AB-AWE-HAH

Aboha can help you when you need to learn effectively, or when you need to pass exams. The best results come when you ask for help at the beginning of your study, but if the exam is looming, you can still ask for help to remain calm, focused, and with a clear memory.

If you are looking for people to join you on your quest for success, Aboha is an angel that helps you meet people who could be helpful to you. They may be supporters or financiers, or something else altogether. It helps if you have a clear vision for success, but you don't need to know what sort of person might be a help. Let the angel surprise you.

If you are working to build a good reputation, as an honest person, Aboha can help people see the good and forget the bad.

The Seal of Aboha

The Sensory Triggers
A lush field illuminated by starlight.
A full white moon in the blue morning sky.

ELL, EE-AH-OH-EH
ELL-OH-HEEM
ELL-SHAD-EYE
ADD-OH-NIGH
AG-AH-LAH
ADD-VAH-KEY-ELL
AB-AWE-HAH

34. The Angel Yasgedibarodiel

Yasgedibarodiel is the Angel of the Third Decan of Capricorn.

The Astrological Correspondence is The Sun in Capricorn.

The day of Yasgedibarodiel is Saturday.

The Ruling Archangel is Haniel.

Haniel is pronounced as
HAH-NEE-ELL

Yasgedibarodiel is pronounced as
YAH-SEH-GEH-DEE-BAR-AWE-DEE-ELL

Yasgedibarodiel is known to assist with health and beauty. This does not mean the angel can cure all illness or make you look twenty years younger, but the powers can be remarkable. If you ask the angel to make you appear more beautiful, you will look more vibrant and alive. If you wish to maintain or recover health, the angel can assist with your efforts.

Yasgedibarodiel can also help you be more attractive to somebody you like, as a potential friend or romantic partner, without deception. Your inner beauty will be made apparent to the other person.

Yasgedibarodiel is powerful in the art of focus, and if you need to master a difficult skill, you can ask for the perception, persistence, and ability to improve that skill.

The Seal of Yasgedibarodiel

The Sensory Triggers
Blue smoke from smoldering embers.
Blue flowers grow from black soil.

ELL, EE-AH-OH-EH
ELL-OH-HEEM
ELL-SHAD-EYE
ADD-OH-NIGH
AG-AH-LAH
HAH-NEE-ELL
YAH-SEH-GEH-DEE-BAR-AWE-DEE-ELL

35. The Angel Gerodiel

Gerodiel is the Angel of the Third Decan of Aquarius.

The Astrological Correspondence is The Moon in Aquarius.

The day of Gerodiel is Saturday.

The Ruling Archangel is Cambriel.

Cambriel is pronounced as
CAM-BREE-ELL

Gerodiel is pronounced as
GEH-RAW-DEE-ELL

Gerodiel can help you recover from overwhelming sorrow. If your sadness is ongoing, you can ask the angel to bring people into your life (or back into your life), to help ease the pain of sorrow. The sorrow may be caused by grief, confusion, or any kind of loss.

Gerodiel can help you settle your emotions without anesthetizing them. If you need a clear head, without being swayed too much by your heart, the angel will help you to remain calm while you deal with difficult situations, complex speculation, or situations that would otherwise be emotionally overwhelming.

The Seal of Gerodiel

The Sensory Triggers
Tiny stars are visible in the blue twilight.
A silver crown on the dark muddy riverbank.

ELL, EE-AH-OH-EH
ELL-OH-HEEM
ELL-SHAD-EYE
ADD-OH-NIGH
AG-AH-LAH
CAM-BREE-ELL
GEH-RAW-DEE-ELL

36. The Angel Satrip

Satrip is the Angel of the Third Decan of Pisces.

The Astrological Correspondence is Mars in Pisces.

The day of Satrip is Monday.

The Ruling Archangel is Amnitziel.

Amnitziel is pronounced as
AM-NEAT-SEE-ELL

Satrip is pronounced as
SAH-TREEP

Satrip is an angel who brings strong feelings of confidence and self-belief. If you need confidence in any situation, or in life generally, this angel can assist.

You can also ask the angel to inspire your musical composition and performance. If your music suffers because of a lack of confidence, this angel could help you to find new depths in your musical ability by building creative courage.

There are many angels that can help you gain clarity about what you want, but Satrip can help you to see what you want in your heart of hearts, in life, love, and any other matter. If you are ready to see how big your dreams might be, ask Satrip to let the revelations begin.

The Seal of Satrip

The Sensory Triggers
A silver sword, glowing with amber flames.
A crackling fire with red flames.

ELL, EE-AH-OH-EH
ELL-OH-HEEM
ELL-SHAD-EYE
ADD-OH-NIGH
AG-AH-LAH
AM-NEAT-SEE-ELL
SAH-TREEP

Pronunciation Guide

Pronouncing these sounds is easy, but even if you make some mistakes, that's going to be ok, because the angelic seal makes the primary connection to the angel.

When you speak, you are echoing the content of the seal. When you use the Sensory Triggers, you are breaking reality apart to reach out to the angel.

The spoken words are important, but you don't need to learn perfect pronunciation. In most cases, these sounds have already been made easier to say for English speakers (because most readers won't know Hebrew), so you can hardly go wrong. And if you do, it won't matter. Be confident, feel the words, and let that energy carry you through the ritual.

Most of the time, these words sound the way they look. ELL is obviously the ELL sound you get in TELL or SELL. EE is obviously the EE sound you get in SEE or FREE. There are a few sounds that you should learn, making the whole process much easier, and I will show them to you.

ER
This is the **ER** sound you get at the end of words like **LETTER**.

AH
The **AH** sound is like the A sound in **FATHER**. You can also say this is like the **A** in **MA** and **PA**. Sometimes an extra letter is added, like **HAH**. This is as easy as adding **H** to the front of the **AH** sound.

AW or AWE
AW is the **AW** sound in **PAW**. There are several occasions where other letters are added, as with the sound **RAWN**. If you know the **AW** sound, it is easy to add those letters. To clarify,

RAWN is like **LAWN** with **R** instead of **L**. **AWE** sounds like the word **AWE**, and is very easy to use.

EH

EH is like the **E** sound in the word **PET**. Sometimes an extra letter is added, as with the **LEH** sound. This is as easy as adding **L** to the front of the **EH** sound.

G

G sounds like the **g** in **glow**, rather than the **g** in **giraffe**.

TS

This comes at the end of words and is the same as the ending of words like **VATS** or **PATS**.

With those examples giving the most important sounds you need, I will now run through the main sounds in the ritual, which will be spoken each time you use this magick. Also, I will use the archangel Malchidiel and the angel Zazer from the first ritual. After reading this, you should be confident enough to use any pronunciation in the book.

ELL, EE-AH-OH-EH

ELL-OH-HEEM

ELL-SHAD-EYE

ADD-OH-NIGH

AG-AH-LAH

MAH-LEH-KEY-DEE-ELL

ZAH-ZER

ELL

As previously mentioned, this is **SELL** without the **S**.

EE-AH-OH-EH

EE is the **EE** sound in **SEE**. **AH** is the **A** sound in **FATHER**. **OH** is the word **OH**. **EH** is the **E** sound in **MET**.

ELL-OH-HEEM
ELL and **OH** should be familiar by now. **HEEM** is like **SEEM**, with **H** instead of **S**.

ELL-SHAD-EYE
ELL is now familiar. **SHAD** is like the first part of **SHADOW**. **EYE** is the word **EYE**.

ADD-OH-NIGH
ADD is the word **ADD**. **OH** is familiar, and **NIGH** is **NIGHT** without the **T**.

AG-AH-LAH
AG is the **AG** sound in **RAG**. **AH** is now familiar. **LAH** is the **AH** sound with an **L**.

MAH-LEH-KEY-DEE-ELL
MAH is **AH** with an **M**. **LEH** is like **LET** without the **T**. **KEY** is the word **KEY**. **DEE** is **DEEP** without the **P**, and **ELL** is familiar.

ZAH-ZER
ZAH is the **AH** sound with a **Z**. **ZER** is the **ER** sound with **Z** at the front, like the end of **LASER**.

That has been broken down into more detail than you will ever need, and you can probably just read the capital letters and see how it's meant to sound. You do run the sounds together, so that ZAH-ZER becomes the one name Zazer, for example. This is quite easy, even with only a small amount of practice.

When you have learned to say the main ritual, you never have much to learn in a day. You might have just the archangel name and the angel name to learn. That could take as little as a minute, or perhaps five minutes to become confident saying the names. It's ok to practice saying all these names out loud because magick doesn't happen without your magickal intent, so saying the words to test the sounds is safe.

Other Associations

What follows is a list of associations for each angel, but I do not believe these are required or particularly useful. As explained earlier, I believe the Tarot may often be misleading, but I include them for the sake of producing a complete text, with details that may interest some readers. A list of gemstones is also included. Each angel is associated with one or more. This has not helped further my magickal connection, and certainly should not be seen as necessary, as acquiring a large collection of gems would be expensive and probably doesn't assist the magick. If, however, you are deeply interested in gemstones already, this may be of some interest to you.

I hope you will see what I give in this book is a complete system and I am only offering these notes should you want to explore, but please remember that even with the help of many wise people, I found these associations add nothing to the magick.

1. The Angel Zazer: Two of Wands. Jasper.
2. The Angel Kadamidi: Five of Pentacles. Rose Quartz.
3. The Angel Sagarash: Eight of Swords. Agate.
4. The Angel Mathravash: Two of Cups. Pearl.
5. The Angel Losanahar: Five of Wands. Onyx.
6. The Angel Ananaurah: Eight of Pentacles. Carnelian.
7. The Angel Tarasni: Two of Swords. Aquamarine.
8. The Angel Kamotz: Five of Cups. Beryl.
9. The Angel Mishrath: Eight of Wands. Topaz.
10. The Angel Misnin: Two of Pentacles. Garnet.
11. The Angel Saspam: Five of Swords. Jasper.
12. The Angel Bihelami: Eight of Cups. Aquamarine.
13. The Angel Behahemi: Three of Wands. Diamond.
14. The Angel Minacharai: Six of Pentacles. Sapphire.
15. The Angel Shehadani: Nine of Swords. Citrine.

16. The Angel Rahadetz: Three of Cups. Moonstone.
17. The Angel Zachi: Six of Wands. Ruby.
18. The Angel Rayadyah: Nine of Pentacles. Sapphire.
19. The Angel Saharnatz: Three of Swords. Agate.
20. The Angel Nundohar: Six of Cups. Topaz.
21. The Angel Vehrin: Nine of Wands. Turquoise.
22. The Angel Yasyasyah: Three of Pentacles. Ruby.
23. The Angel Abdaron: Six of Swords. Garnet.
24. The Angel Avron: Nine of Cups. Amethyst.
25. The Angel Satonder: Four of Wands. Sapphire.
26. The Angel Yakasaganotz: Seven of Pentacles. Emerald.
27. The Angel Bethon: Ten of Swords. Emerald.
28. The Angel Alinkir: Four of Cups. Ruby.
29. The Angel Sahiber: Seven of Wands. Sardonyx.
30. The Angel Mishpar: Ten of Pentacles. Peridot.
31. The Angel Shachdar: Four of Swords. Sapphire.
32. The Angel Uthrodiel: Seven of Cups. Citrine.
33. The Angel Aboha: Ten of Wands. Ruby.
34. The Angel Yasgedibarodiel: Four of Pentacles. Emerald.
35. The Angel Gerodiel: Seven of Swords. Quartz.
36. The Angel Satrip: Ten of Cups. Bloodstone.

Towards a Bibliography

I cannot offer a sensible bibliography because my reading and study have taken place over notebooks, in libraries, in the company of those who passed on secrets to me verbally, and in more books than I could successfully list. I apologize if further reading is important to you, but my purpose was to provide you with a book of practical magick, and I put all other considerations aside.

If you want to know the sort of books I was looking through, welcome to a glimpse of a tiny portion of my personal library, which was out on the research shelf during the last week of fact-checking.

That's a fraction of my collection. Although valuable, all are worthless unless the magickal knowledge gleaned from them is connected to the larger context of work by occultists who have interpreted this particular magick with the Angels of The Decans.

If you are looking for further reading and information on these angels, I suggest that you may not find much information in any single volume. In books such as *The Complete Magician's Tables* by Stephen Skinner, or Aleister Crowley's *Liber 777,* you will find a list of the angels, but no detail. Other writers (some more obscure; some writing documents that formed part of a secret order's hidden oeuvre) cannot be listed for obvious reasons.

It's taken me five years to untangle this mystery, and each book contains only an infinitesimal preview of the complete knowledge. The bigger picture is *this* book.

To those with academic inclinations I feel guilty for not keeping track of more thorough references as I wrote, but although I consider myself a keen-eyed and creative researcher, I am not an academic and if you want to go into academic study on this subject then I believe you will know how to find what you need with great ease and without my guidance.

For most readers, it's all about the practice. Perform the magick and enjoy it with ease and gratitude, and you will become somebody who knows magick, with power over the waves of Fortune.

I would like to offer Grateful Thanks to you for putting your trust in this book and giving the magick a chance to work. I will share the energy of my magick with everybody who has purchased this book and hope I can empower you further. Gratitude is an energy that brings change, and I feel grateful to you for having shared in this journey and for trusting in the truth of my book. I believe it will work for you as I have witnessed it work so often for myself, and for those I know and love.

Rose Manning

CPSIA information can be obtained
at www.ICGtesting.com
Printed in the USA
FSHW021949080919
61821FS